BELIEVE IN
yourself

Girls
GRATITUDE
JOURNAL

THIS JOURNAL BELONGS TO:

My name is:

- - - - - - - - - - - - - - - -

I am_____years old

I live in

- - - - - - - - - - - - - - - -

My signature

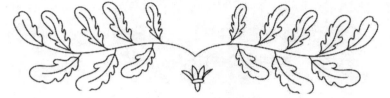

My Favorite Books

HELLO THERE.

I WANT YOU TO KNOW THAT YOU ARE A UNIQUE AND POWERFUL BEING WITH MUCH TO OFFER THE WORLD.

YOU HAVE THE POTENTIAL TO MAKE A DIFFERENCE AND ARE DESTINED FOR GREATNESS.

DON'T GIVE UP ON YOUR DREAMS, AND ALWAYS REMEMBER HOW SPECIAL AND UNIQUE YOU ARE.

THANK YOU FOR BEING YOU.

In this journal, you can write about anything you're grateful for. Consider your family, friends, pets, and all the other beautiful aspects of your life.

Beginning each day by reflecting on the things you are grateful for can set a positive and contented tone for the rest of the day.

Once you finish writing, you can engage in the relaxing activity of coloring. There are many fun and intricate designs to choose from that will help you focus and be present in the moment.

In addition to writing about the things you are grateful for, you can also use this journal as a space to express any challenges or problems you are facing and how they are making you feel.

It can be therapeutic to express yourself openly, and you may even discover some solutions to your problems.

If you happen to miss a day of writing, don't worry. Just continue the next day and remember to enjoy this new journey.

WHAT IS MINDFULNESS?

MINDFULNESS IS THE ACT OF BRINGING AWARENESS TO THE PRESENT MOMENT AND PAYING ATTENTION TO ONE'S THOUGHTS, FEELINGS, AND SURROUNDINGS.
IT IS NOT ABOUT REACHING A SPECIFIC STATE OF PEACE OR SERENITY; RATHER, IT IS ABOUT ACKNOWLEDGING AND ACCEPTING YOUR CURRENT EXPERIENCE WITH OPENNESS AND COMPASSION.

BODY SCAN MEDITATION IS A HELPFUL TECHNIQUE FOR BRINGING YOUR ATTENTION TO THE PRESENT MOMENT, ESPECIALLY WHEN YOU FEEL OVERWHELMED BY YOUR THOUGHTS AND EMOTIONS. IT INVOLVES FOCUSING ON THE SENSATIONS IN YOUR BODY AND BRINGING A SENSE OF CALM, ATTENTION, AND APPRECIATION TO YOUR DAILY OR EVENING ROUTINE.

MINDFULNESS PRACTICE

MINDFUL BREATHING

FOCUS ON YOUR BREATH AND THE SENSATION OF THE AIR MOVING THROUGH YOUR BODY. YOU CAN ADD WORDS OR VISUALIZATIONS TO THE PRACTICE TO MAKE IT MORE IMMERSIVE AND ENGAGING.

BELLY BREATHING

FOCUS ON THE MOVEMENT OF YOUR STOMACH AS YOU INHALE AND EXHALE. NOTICE HOW THE STOMACH EXPANDS SLIGHTLY ON INHALATION AND CONTRACTS ON EXHALATION. PRACTICE THIS FOR A FEW BREATHS, THEN RETURN TO NORMAL BREATHING.

MINDFUL TIPS

1. Accept imperfection

2. Listen with curiosity

3. Communicate with courage

4. Practice gratitude and appreciation

5. Forgive yourself and others

6. Practice support and generosity

7. Remember to Play and Have Fun

ARE YOU HAPPY WITH HOW TODAY TURNED OUT?

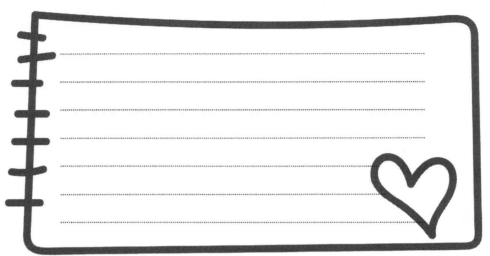

What have you learned about yourself today?

COLOR THE FACE THAT BEST DESCRIBES YOUR MOOD TODAY.

I AM FEELING.. DATE ___ / ___ / ___

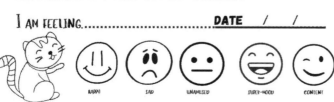

HAPPY   SAD   UNAMUSED   SUPER-MOOD   CONTENT

I ALWAYS GIVE MY ALL TO EVERYTHING I DO.

Think about the qualities
of the people you admire.
List these qualities and
how you
can incorporate them
into your life.

**COLOR THE FACE THAT BEST
DESCRIBES YOUR MOOD TODAY.**

I AM FEELING....................... DATE   /   /

HAPPY   SAD   UNAMUSED   SUPER-HOOU   CONTENT

TODAY IS A BLESSING BECAUSE... _____

_____

_____

_____

Let's make today beautiful

COLOR THE FACE THAT BEST DESCRIBES YOUR MOOD TODAY.

I AM FEELING.................................... DATE ___ / ___ / ___

HAPPY

SAD

UNAMUSED

SUPER-MOOD

CONTENT

I have the courage to be myself.

WHAT'S YOUR FAVORITE THING ABOUT YOURSELF, AND WHY?

COLOR THE FACE THAT BEST DESCRIBES YOUR MOOD TODAY.

I AM FEELING.................... DATE / /

HAPPY   SAD   UNAMUSED   SUPER-MOOD   CONTENT

TODAY IS GOING TO BE FANTASTIC

BECAUSE...

Name three things that you are grateful for.

COLOR THE FACE THAT BEST
DESCRIBES YOUR MOOD TODAY.

I AM FEELING.................................. DATE   /   /

HAPPY   SAD   UNAMUSED   SUPER-MOOD   CONTENT

I AM HAPPY

COLOR YOUR WAY
TO HAPPINESS.

COLOR THE FACE THAT BEST
DESCRIBES YOUR MOOD TODAY.

I AM FEELING......................... DATE / /

HAPPY   SAD   UNAMUSED   SUPER-MOOD   CONTENT

There are many things to be grateful for, even the small things we often take for granted. Experiencing the good moments in life can be a great way to remind yourself of all the positives, no matter how big or small they may be.

One good thing that happened today...

o - _____

o - _____

o - _____

COLOR THE FACE THAT BEST DESCRIBES YOUR MOOD TODAY.

I AM FEELING................................. DATE   /   /

HAPPY   SAD   UNAMUSED   SUPER-MOOD   CONTENT

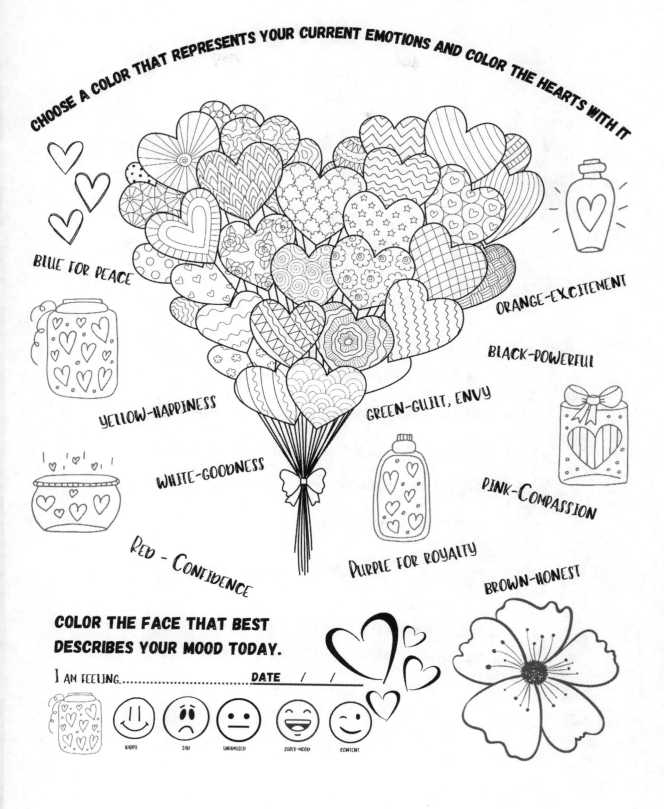

CHOOSE A COLOR THAT REPRESENTS YOUR CURRENT EMOTIONS AND COLOR THE HEARTS WITH IT

BLUE FOR PEACE

ORANGE-EXCITEMENT

BLACK-POWERFUL

YELLOW-HAPPINESS

GREEN-GUILT, ENVY

WHITE-GOODNESS

PINK-COMPASSION

RED - CONFIDENCE

PURPLE FOR ROYALTY

BROWN-HONEST

COLOR THE FACE THAT BEST
DESCRIBES YOUR MOOD TODAY.

I AM FEELING........................ DATE __/__/__

HAPPY   SAD   UNAMUSED   SUPER-NOOD   CONTENT

- SIT COMFORTABLY AND CLOSE YOUR EYES.

- TAKE A DEEP BREATH AND RELAX YOUR BODY.

- VISUALIZE A BRIGHT LIGHT IN THE CENTER OF YOUR CHEST.

- ALLOW THE LIGHT TO GROW UNTIL IT FILLS YOUR ENTIRE BODY.

- HOLD THE LIGHT FOR A FEW MOMENTS AND THEN RELEASE IT.

- REPEAT THE PROCESS A FEW TIMES

COLOR THE FACE THAT BEST DESCRIBES YOUR MOOD TODAY.

I AM FEELING.......................... DATE   /   /

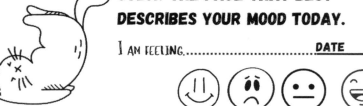

HAPPY   SAD   UNAMUSED   SUPER-MOOD   CONTENT

IMAGINE THIS TO BE A MAGICAL TREE THAT WILL GRANT ALL OF YOUR WISHES AND DESIRES.

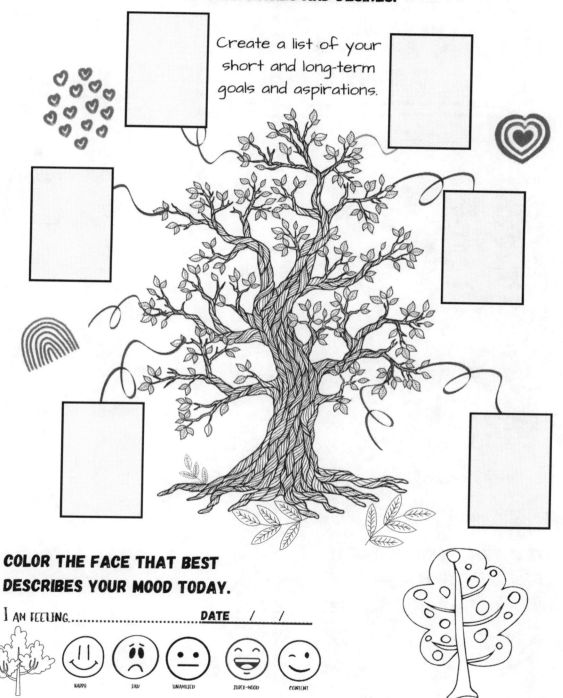

Create a list of your short and long-term goals and aspirations.

COLOR THE FACE THAT BEST DESCRIBES YOUR MOOD TODAY.

I AM FEELING.............................. DATE / /

HAPPY   SAD   UNAMUSED   SUPER-MOOD   CONTENT

WRITE DOWN EVERY GOOD THING THAT HAS HAPPENED TO YOU TODAY.

COLOR THE FACE THAT BEST DESCRIBES YOUR MOOD TODAY.

I AM FEELING.. DATE   /   /

HAPPY   SAD   UNAMUSED   SUPER-MOOD   CONTENT

A GREAT WAY TO TURN YOUR DREAMS INTO REALITY IS TO PUT THEM IN WRITING. MAKE A LIST OF YOUR TOP FIVE WISHES AND START TAKING STEPS TOWARDS MAKING EACH ONE COME TRUE.

COLOR THE FACE THAT BEST DESCRIBES YOUR MOOD TODAY.

I AM FEELING................................ DATE   /   /

HAPPY   SAD   UNAMUSED   SUPER-GOOD   CONTENT

my life is a beautiful ride

WHICH PARTS OF YOUR UPBRINGING DO YOU VALUE THE MOST?

_____

_____

_____

_____

_____

COLOR THE FACE THAT BEST DESCRIBES YOUR MOOD TODAY.

I AM FEELING.................................. DATE   /   /

HAPPY   SAD   UNAMUSED   SUPER-MOOD   CONTENT

I AM GRATEFUL FOR:

....

....

....

....

ARE YOU HAPPY WITH HOW THE DAY HAS GONE?

....

....

....

**COLOR THE FACE THAT BEST
DESCRIBES YOUR MOOD TODAY.**

I AM FEELING...................................... DATE __/__/__

HAPPY   SAD   UNAMUSED   SUPER-HOOD   CONTENT

WRITE ABOUT SOMETHING POSITIVE YOU DID AND HOW IT MADE YOU FEEL.

COLOR THE FACE THAT BEST
DESCRIBES YOUR MOOD TODAY.

I AM FEELING.................................. DATE   /   /

HAPPY   SAD   UNAMUSED   SUPER-MOOD   CONTENT

In your opinion, what are three things that you're currently doing exceptionally well?

_____

_____

_____

_____

COLOR THE FACE THAT BEST DESCRIBES YOUR MOOD TODAY.

I AM FEELING.................... DATE / /

HAPPY   SAD   UNAMUSED   SUPER-GOOD   CONTENT

Can you think of one thing that went well or was particularly enjoyable today? It could be something small or something more significant. Reflecting on the good things in our lives can help us cultivate a more positive and grateful perspective.

_____

_____

_____

_____

COLOR THE FACE THAT BEST DESCRIBES YOUR MOOD TODAY.

I AM FEELING........................... DATE ___ / ___ / ___

HAPPY   SAD   UNAMUSED   SUPER-MOOD   CONTENT

**COLOR THE FACE THAT BEST
DESCRIBES YOUR MOOD TODAY.**

I AM FEELING.................................. **DATE** ___/___/___

HAPPY   SAD   UNAMUSED   SUPER-MOOD   CONTENT

Take a moment to write down your worries or fears in these bubbles.

Close your eyes and take a deep breath in, filling your lungs with fresh air.

As you exhale, imagine the bubbles lifting your worries and fears away, carrying them into the sky.

With each breath you take, feel your worries drifting further away, leaving you feeling calm and at peace.

Imagine yourself surrounded by a sense of tranquility and serenity.

Keep breathing in peace and exhaling worries until you feel your mind and body fully relaxed.

BLOW YOUR WORRIES AWAY

**COLOR THE FACE THAT BEST
DESCRIBES YOUR MOOD TODAY.**

I AM FEELING.............................. DATE   /   /

HAPPY   SAD   UNAMUSED   SUPER-MOOD   CONTENT

Who do you find yourself having the most fun with when you have free time? Reflect on their impact on your life and how much they mean to you. Consider writing a heartfelt letter to express your gratitude for their friendship and how much they mean to you. Once you've finished, take the time to give it to them and bring a smile to their face.

COLOR THE FACE THAT BEST DESCRIBES YOUR MOOD TODAY.

I AM FEELING.................................. DATE   /   /

HAPPY   SAD   UNAMUSED   SUPER-MOOD   CONTENT

GIVE THANKS FOR THE THING(S) YOU VALUE MOST IN YOUR LIFE.

COLOR THE FACE THAT BEST
DESCRIBES YOUR MOOD TODAY.

I AM FEELING.................................. DATE / /

HAPPY   SAD   UNAMUSED   SUPER-MOOD   CONTENT

WHAT IS SOMETHING YOU RECENTLY DID THAT WAS DIFFERENT OR CHALLENGING FOR YOU?

_____

_____

_____

COLOR THE FACE THAT BEST DESCRIBES YOUR MOOD TODAY.

I AM FEELING................................ DATE ___/___/___

HAPPY   SAD   UNAMUSED   SUPER-MOOD   CONTENT

Did anything unexpected or unusual occur this week? If so, how did you react at the moment?

Writing about the event can be a helpful way to remember the details and process any emotions you may have had about it.

journal

- _____
- _____
- _____
- _____
- _____
- _____

COLOR THE FACE THAT BEST DESCRIBES YOUR MOOD TODAY.

I AM FEELING.................................... DATE   /   /

HAPPY   SAD   UNAMUSED   SUPER-HOOD   CONTENT

COLOR THE FACE THAT BEST DESCRIBES YOUR MOOD TODAY.

I AM FEELING.............................. DATE ___ / ___ / ___

HAPPY SAD UNAMUSED SUPER-MOOD CONTENT

Doing something good for others can be extremely rewarding. Whether it's by helping a friend in need or positively impacting the world, there are many ways to spread cheer and positivity.

Can you come up with an idea of how you can show kindness to someone the next time an opportunity presents itself?

WHAT'S SOMETHING NEW THAT YOU LEARNED TODAY?

COLOR THE FACE THAT BEST DESCRIBES YOUR MOOD TODAY.

I AM FEELING.................................... DATE   /   /

HAPPY   SAD   UNAMUSED   SUPER-MOOD   CONTENT

Some memories or thoughts stay with us for too long, even though we know they make us sad.

There will be a time when we have to let go and feel free, whether it's a bad habit, a negative way of thinking, or even just an attachment to something material.

Is there something that's stopping you from moving forward or something that doesn't make you happy anymore?

Can you write about how you think you'd feel if you let go of it?

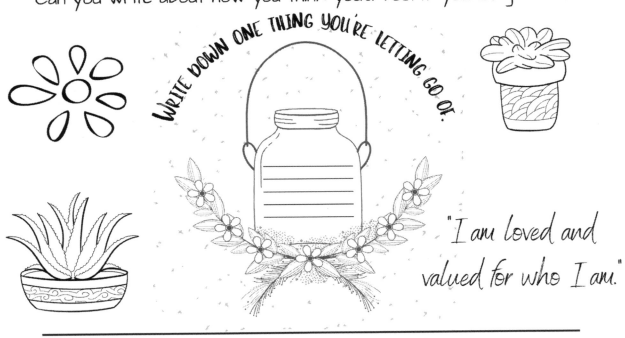

WRITE DOWN ONE THING YOU'RE LETTING GO OF.

"I am loved and valued for who I am."

_____

_____

COLOR THE FACE THAT BEST DESCRIBES YOUR MOOD TODAY.

I AM FEELING... DATE ___/___/___

HAPPY · SAD · UNAMUSED · SUPER-MOOD · CONTENT

COLOR THE FACE THAT BEST DESCRIBES YOUR MOOD TODAY.

I AM FEELING.................................... DATE   /   /

HAPPY   SAD   UNAMUSED   SUPER-MOOD   CONTENT

WHAT DO YOU LIKE THE MOST ABOUT YOURSELF?

_____

_____

_____

_____

_____

_____

"Beautiful people are not always good, but good people are always beautiful"

-IMAN ALI

When your self-esteem is low, write yourself some encouraging words.

HERE ARE A FEW EXAMPLES:

- " I have the ability to learn and grow from every experience."
- "I am unique and valuable, just as I am."
- "I control my thoughts and actions, and I choose to use them positively."
- _____

_____

_____

COLOR THE FACE THAT BEST DESCRIBES YOUR MOOD TODAY.

I AM FEELING.. DATE ___/___/___

HAPPY   SAD   UNAMUSED   SUPER-MOOD   CONTENT

COLOR THE FACE THAT BEST DESCRIBES YOUR MOOD TODAY.

I AM FEELING.................................... DATE ___ / ___ / ___

HAPPY · SAD · UNAMUSED · SUPER-MOOD · CONTENT

Don't Forget To Be Awesome

IF YOUR BEST FRIENDS HAD TO DESCRIBE YOU IN A FEW WORDS, WHAT DO YOU THINK THEY WOULD SAY?

_____

_____

_____

_____

Reflect on a past experience that affected you deeply.
Consider the emotions it triggered and why. Write about
your feelings and thoughts during the event and whether
you would have acted differently.
Understanding our reactions can lead to self-awareness
and personal growth.

_____

_____

_____

_____

COLOR THE FACE THAT BEST
DESCRIBES YOUR MOOD TODAY.

I AM FEELING.............................. DATE ___/___/___

HAPPY   SAD   UNAMUSED   SUPER-MOOD   CONTENT

WHO IN YOUR FAMILY HOLDS A SPECIAL PLACE IN YOUR HEART, AND WHY?

COLOR THE FACE THAT BEST DESCRIBES YOUR MOOD TODAY.

I AM FEELING.................................... DATE   /   /

HAPPY   SAD   UNAMUSED   SUPER-MOOD   CONTENT

Are there any particular talents or hobbies you would like to improve upon? What steps can you take to begin working towards bettering yourself in those areas?

_____

_____

_____

_____

_____

_____

_____

_____

COLOR THE FACE THAT BEST DESCRIBES YOUR MOOD TODAY.

I AM FEELING.................................... DATE ___/___/___

HAPPY   SAD   UNAMUSED   SUPER-MOOD   CONTENT

Start The DAY with a Smile

COLOR THE FACE THAT BEST DESCRIBES YOUR MOOD TODAY.

I AM FEELING.................................... DATE   /   /

HAPPY   SAD   UNAMUSED   SUPER-MOOD   CONTENT

WHAT IS YOUR FAVORITE THING TO DO? WHAT DO YOU LOVE MOST ABOUT IT?

_ _

_ _

_ _

_ _

_ _

_ _

_ _

What are some ways you can contribute to someone else's happiness or well-being?

COLOR THE FACE THAT BEST DESCRIBES YOUR MOOD TODAY.

I AM FEELING..................................... DATE   /   /

HAPPY   SAD   UNAMUSED   SUPER-MOOD   CONTENT

Think about something that makes you special and unique. What are the things you like most about yourself? How do these things make you feel good about who you are?

_____

_____

_____

_____

_____

_____

COLOR THE FACE THAT BEST DESCRIBES YOUR MOOD TODAY.

I AM FEELING................._____ DATE __/__/__

HAPPY   SAD   UNAMUSED   SUPER-MOOD   CONTENT

COLOR THE FACE THAT BEST DESCRIBES YOUR MOOD TODAY.

I AM FEELING.................................... DATE / /

HAPPY   SAD   UNAMUSED   SUPER-MOOD   CONTENT

Todo

Who has taught you the true meaning of unconditional love, either in the past or present?

1 ....

2 ....

3 ....

4 ....

Love

WHAT IS A PLACE WHERE YOU FEEL MOST COMFORTABLE BEING YOURSELF?

_____

_____

How does this place make you feel, and what is it about this place that allows you to be yourself?

_____

_____

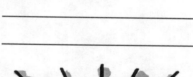

COLOR THE FACE THAT BEST DESCRIBES YOUR MOOD TODAY.

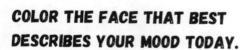

I AM FEELING.......................... DATE / /

HAPPY

SAD

UNAMUSED

SUPER-MOOD

CONTENT

DRAW A PICTURE OF SOMETHING THAT BRINGS YOU CALM AND PEACE, SUCH AS A PERSON, PLACE, OR OBJECT.

COLOR THE FACE THAT BEST DESCRIBES YOUR MOOD TODAY.

I AM FEELING.................................... DATE ___ / ___ / ___

HAPPY   SAD   UNAMUSED   SUPER-MOOD   CONTENT

COLOR THE FACE THAT BEST DESCRIBES YOUR MOOD TODAY.

I AM FEELING............................ DATE / /

HAPPY   SAD   UNAMUSED   SUPER-MOOD   CONTENT

WRITE ABOUT AN ACTIVITY THAT BROUGHT YOU JOY THIS WEEK.

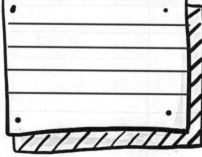

WRITE ABOUT A PROUD MOMENT THAT YOU HAD THIS WEEK.

_____

_____

_____

_____

COLOR THE FACE THAT BEST DESCRIBES YOUR MOOD TODAY.

I AM FEELING.............................. DATE   /   /   _____

HAPPY   SAD   UNAMUSED   SUPER-HOOD   CONTENT

"MINDFULNESS ISN'T DIFFICULT: WE JUST NEED TO REMEMBER TO DO IT."
~SHARON SALZBERG

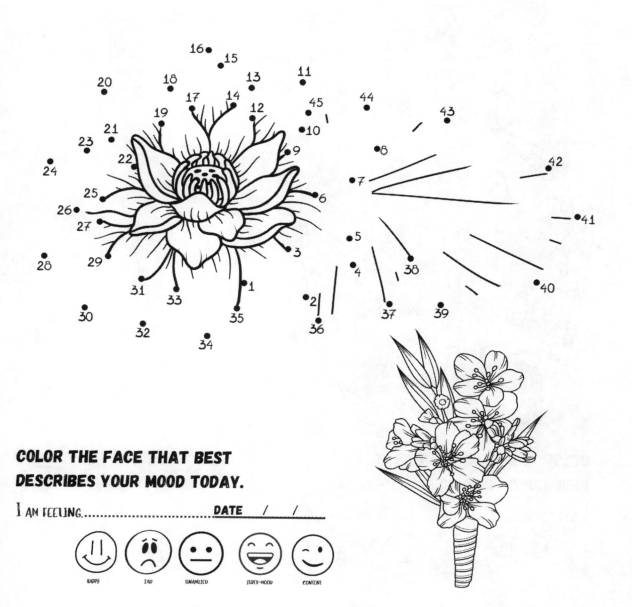

COLOR THE FACE THAT BEST DESCRIBES YOUR MOOD TODAY.

I AM FEELING................................. DATE / /

HAPPY   SAD   UNAMUSED   SUPER-MOOD   CONTENT

Think about people or things in your life that you may take for granted and come up with ways to show more appreciation for them.

_____

_____

_____

_____

COLOR THE FACE THAT BEST DESCRIBES YOUR MOOD TODAY.

I AM FEELING.................................... DATE ___/___/___

HAPPY   SAD   UNAMUSED   SUPER-MOOD   CONTENT

Take some time to think about the unique qualities and characteristics that make your friends special to you. Appreciating your friends and the positive impact they have on your life can be a fun and uplifting activity that helps you feel grateful for their friendship.

COLOR THE FACE THAT BEST
DESCRIBES YOUR MOOD TODAY.

I AM FEELING... DATE   /   /

HAPPY   SAD   UNAMUSED   SUPER-MOOD   CONTENT

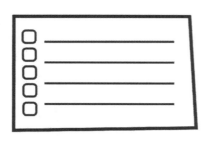

Think about the qualities and characteristics you admire in each of your teachers and write them down.

This can be a meaningful way to show your appreciation for them.

_____

_____

_____

_____

_____

_____

_____

_____

_____

_____

_____

What is something that you have learned in the past that has helped you grow as a person?

my life is a beautiful ride

COLOR THE FACE THAT BEST DESCRIBES YOUR MOOD TODAY.

I AM FEELING............................... DATE   /   /

HAPPY   SAD   UNAMUSED   SUPER-GOOD   CONTENT

THERE ARE VARIOUS WAYS YOU CAN BRING POSITIVE ENERGY INTO YOUR LIFE.

_____

_____

_____

One way is to start each day with a positive thought.
Another is to do something that brings you joy and makes you feel good every day.
You can also surround yourself with people who are kind and make you feel good about yourself.
Lastly, you can visualize yourself surrounded by good energy.

COLOR THE FACE THAT BEST DESCRIBES YOUR MOOD TODAY.

I AM FEELING.............................. DATE / /

HAPPY   SAD   UNAMUSED   SUPER-MOOD   CONTENT

HAVE YOU EVER EXPERIENCED NEGATIVE EMOTIONS DUE TO SOMEONE'S WORDS OR ACTIONS OR A SPECIFIC EVENT OR SITUATION?

IF YES, HOW DID THAT MAKE YOU FEEL?

One effective way to process your emotions is to identify and acknowledge them and then consider expressing them through writing. It can be a beneficial and therapeutic way to process your feelings and gain insight into your thoughts and experiences."

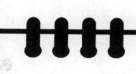

COLOR THE FACE THAT BEST DESCRIBES YOUR MOOD TODAY.

 I AM FEELING.................................... DATE / /

HAPPY   SAD   UNAMUSED   SUPER-MOOD   CONTENT

WHAT HABITS ABOUT YOURSELF WOULD YOU CHANGE, AND WHY?

There are certain habits that everyone would like to improve upon, and it takes effort and commitment to make those changes. However, by consistently practicing new behaviors and patterns, you can bring about positive changes in yourself and your life. Keep in mind that change takes time and requires persistence, but all of the effort is worth it in the end when you see the positive impact it has on your personal growth and well-being. Remember to be patient and give yourself credit for your progress.

_____

_____

_____

_____

COLOR THE FACE THAT BEST DESCRIBES YOUR MOOD TODAY.

I AM FEELING.. DATE ____ / ____ / ____

HAPPY   SAD   UNAMUSED   SUPER-MOOD   CONTENT

What is something that you feel proud of accomplishing or overcoming? How did you navigate through that challenge, and what did you learn from it?

_____

_____

_____

_____

_____

Never stop dreaming

COLOR THE FACE THAT BEST DESCRIBES YOUR MOOD TODAY.

I AM FEELING.............................. **DATE** / /

HAPPY SAD UNAMUSED SUPER-MOOD CONTENT

WRITE ABOUT ANY THOUGHTS, IDEAS, OR FEELINGS YOU WANT TO EXPRESS OR SHARE.

_____

_____

_____

COLOR THE FACE THAT BEST
DESCRIBES YOUR MOOD TODAY.

I AM FEELING...................................... DATE ___ / ___ / ___

HAPPY   SAD   UNAMUSED   SUPER-MOOD   CONTENT

My heart is filled with...

_____

_____

_____

Expressing gratitude can transform our perspective and bring more positivity into our lives. When we take time to appreciate the things that bring us happiness, our hearts are filled with love, gratitude, and joy. Even on difficult days, focusing on what we are thankful for can help us find ways to bring more positivity into our lives. By cultivating a grateful heart, we can live more fulfilling and meaningful lives.

COLOR THE FACE THAT BEST DESCRIBES YOUR MOOD TODAY.

I AM FEELING.......................... DATE ___ / ___ / ___

 HAPPY
 SAD
 UNAMUSED
 SUPER-MOOD
 CONTENT

WHAT SUBJECT OR TOPIC ARE YOU INTERESTED IN EXPLORING OR LEARNING MORE ABOUT?

COLOR THE FACE THAT BEST
DESCRIBES YOUR MOOD TODAY.

I AM FEELING.. DATE ___ / ___ / ___

HAPPY   SAD   UNAMUSED   SUPER-MOOD   CONTENT

WHAT IS THE MOST MEANINGFUL OR IMPACTFUL EVENT THAT HAS OCCURRED IN YOUR LIFE?

_____

_____

_____

COLOR THE FACE THAT BEST DESCRIBES YOUR MOOD TODAY.

I AM FEELING.............................. DATE   /   /

HAPPY   SAD   UNAMUSED   SUPER-MOOD   CONTENT

WHAT DO YOU HAVE A NATURAL TALENT FOR?

_____

_____

_____

_____

"Be the change that you wish to see in the world."
- Mahatma Gandhi

COLOR THE FACE THAT BEST DESCRIBES YOUR MOOD TODAY.

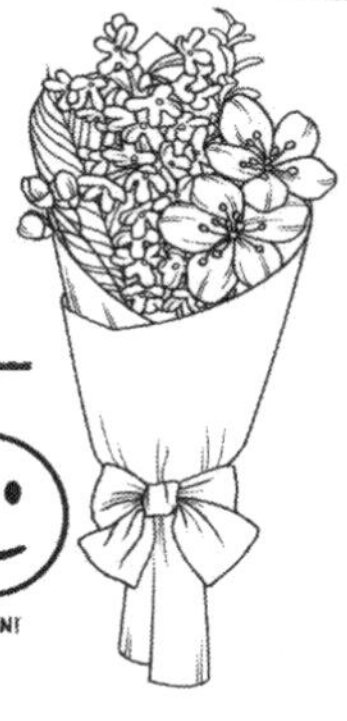

I AM FEELING.. DATE ___ / ___ / ___

HAPPY   SAD   UNAMUSED   SUPER-MOOD   CONTENT

Take a moment to reflect on your most positive or admirable qualities.
Why do these qualities matter to you, and how do they shape who you are as a person?

1.

_____
_____
_____
_____

"I am unique and special just as I am."

2.

3.

COLOR THE FACE THAT BEST DESCRIBES YOUR MOOD TODAY.

I AM FEELING.............................. DATE   /   /

HAPPY   SAD   UNAMUSED   SUPER-MOOD   CONTENT

WHAT ARE SOME SMALL, EVERYDAY THINGS THAT BRING YOU JOY OR CONTENTMENT?

"I'm grateful for this moment of peace and tranquility in my day."

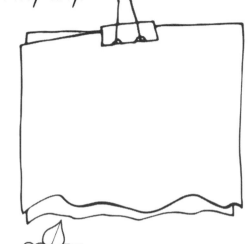

"I continue to improve every day."

COLOR THE FACE THAT BEST DESCRIBES YOUR MOOD TODAY.

I AM FEELING................................ **DATE** ___/___/___

HAPPY   SAD   UNAMUSED   SUPER-MOOD   CONTENT

I can't wait to

"I'm a truly wonderful person."

COLOR THE FACE THAT BEST DESCRIBES YOUR MOOD TODAY.

I AM FEELING.............................. **DATE** / /

HAPPY   SAD   UNAMUSED   SUPER-MOOD   CONTENT

_____

_____

_____

_____

"I am capable of solving my problems."

**COLOR THE FACE THAT BEST
DESCRIBES YOUR MOOD TODAY.**

I AM FEELING......................... DATE ___ / ___ / ___

HAPPY   SAD   UNAMUSED   SUPER-MOOD   CONTENT

There are things we do every day that we may want to change to make our lives better. These changes take time and effort, but they can have a positive impact on our growth and well-being. It's important to be patient and keep trying, even if it's hard.

WHAT PART OF YOUR DAILY ROUTINE DO YOU THINK YOU COULD IMPROVE?

_____

_____

_____

COLOR THE FACE THAT BEST DESCRIBES YOUR MOOD TODAY.

I AM FEELING......................... **DATE** ___/___/___

HAPPY   SAD   UNAMUSED   SUPER-GOOD   CONTENT

"Today, I am a leader."

_____

_____

_____

"I forgive myself for my mistakes."

COLOR THE FACE THAT BEST
DESCRIBES YOUR MOOD TODAY.

I AM FEELING.................................. DATE ___/___/___

HAPPY   SAD   UNAMUSED   SUPER-MOOD   CONTENT

Forgiving someone who has hurt you in the past can be challenging, but it can also be transformative. When you forgive someone, you let go of anger, resentment, and other negative emotions that are holding you back.

You also allow yourself to move on and create a better future.

_____

_____

_____

_____

_____

IMAGINE FORGIVING SOMEONE WHO HURT YOU IN THE PAST. HOW WOULD YOUR LIFE BE DIFFERENT? WHAT WOULD CHANGE?

COLOR THE FACE THAT BEST DESCRIBES YOUR MOOD TODAY.

I AM FEELING............................... DATE ___ / ___ / ___

HAPPY   SAD   UNAMUSED   SUPER-MOOD   CONTENT

"My challenges help me grow."

COLOR THE FACE THAT BEST
DESCRIBES YOUR MOOD TODAY.

I AM FEELING................................ DATE   /   /

HAPPY   SAD   UNAMUSED   SUPER-MOOD   CONTENT

WHAT ARE A FEW ACTIVITIES THAT YOU AND YOUR FRIENDS ENJOY DOING TOGETHER?

_____

_____

_____

_____

Cats

COLOR THE FACE THAT BEST DESCRIBES YOUR MOOD TODAY.

I AM FEELING.............................. DATE   /   /

HAPPY

SAD

UNAMUSED

SUPER-MOOD

CONTENT

Name a few people who are close to you and whom you can always count on to be there for you.

- ○ _____
- ○ _____
- ○ _____
- ○ _____
- ○ _____
- ○ _____
- ○ _____
- ○ _____
- ○ _____

COLOR THE FACE THAT BEST DESCRIBES YOUR MOOD TODAY.

I AM FEELING.................................... DATE ___ / ___ / ___

HAPPY   SAD   UNAMUSED   SUPER-NOOU   CONTENT

Singing has the ability to bring happiness and lift your spirits. It can help you forget about your worries and stress and bring you into a state of mindfulness and peace. The next time you're feeling down, try singing your favorite song and see how it affects your mood.

What is your favorite song!

COLOR THE FACE THAT BEST DESCRIBES YOUR MOOD TODAY.

I AM FEELING.. **DATE** __/__/__

HAPPY

SAD

UNAMUSED

SUPER-MOOD

CONTENT

COLOR THE FACE THAT BEST DESCRIBES YOUR MOOD TODAY.

I AM FEELING.................................... DATE ___/___/___

HAPPY   SAD   UNAMUSED   SUPER-MOOD   CONTENT

COLOR THE FACE THAT BEST DESCRIBES YOUR MOOD TODAY.

I AM FEELING..................................... DATE __/__/__

HAPPY SAD UNANALISED SUPER-MOOD CONTENT

WRITE THE FIRST LETTERS OF THE NAMES OF PEOPLE WHO ARE IMPORTANT TO YOU IN THE TREE OF HEARTS.

THE TREE OF HEARTS

WRITE ABOUT THE PEOPLE IN YOUR LIFE WHOM YOU CAN TURN TO WHEN YOU ARE EXPERIENCING STRONG EMOTIONS AND NEED SOMEONE TO TALK TO.

_____
_____
_____
_____
_____
_____
_____
_____
_____
_____
_____
_____
_____
_____

CIRCLE OF TRUST.

COLOR THE FACE THAT BEST DESCRIBES YOUR MOOD TODAY.

I AM FEELING................................ DATE   /   /

HAPPY   SAD   UNAMUSED   SUPER-MOOD   CONTENT

Think back to a time in the recent past when you did something kind for someone else, whether it was today or earlier this week. It doesn't need to be something magnificent, something as simple as making them smile or feel appreciated can be enough. You may have assisted a friend, held the door open for someone or complimented a friend on their appearance. Reflect on the satisfaction you feel when you help others and how good it makes you feel.

COLOR THE FACE THAT BEST DESCRIBES YOUR MOOD TODAY.

I AM FEELING... DATE ___ / ___ / ___

HAPPY   SAD   UNAMUSED   SUPER-MOOD   CONTENT

WHO IS YOUR GO-TO PERSON FOR SUPPORT?
TELL THEM HOW MUCH THEIR HELP MEANS TO YOU.

_____

_____

_____

_____

COLOR THE FACE THAT BEST
DESCRIBES YOUR MOOD TODAY.

I AM FEELING.......................... DATE ___ / ___ / ___

HAPPY   SAD   UNAMUSED   SUPER-HOOD   CONTENT

COLOR THE FACE THAT BEST
DESCRIBES YOUR MOOD TODAY.

I AM FEELING.............................. **DATE** / /

HAPPY   SAD   UNAMUSED   SUPER-MOOD   CONTENT

What is something that you are passionate about, and how does it bring joy and meaning to your life?

_____

_____

_____

_____

_____

_____

_____

_____

_____

_____

Writing can be a fun and insightful way to explore your thoughts and feelings.
It allows you to discover new perspectives and potentially leads to personal growth and self-discovery. Give it a try and see where your writing takes you.

COLOR THE FACE THAT BEST DESCRIBES YOUR MOOD TODAY.

I AM FEELING............................... DATE   /   /

HAPPY   SAD   UNAMUSED   SUPER-MOOD   CONTENT

COLOR THE FACE THAT BEST DESCRIBES YOUR MOOD TODAY.

I AM FEELING.................................. DATE ___ / ___ / ___

HAPPY   SAD   UNANALISED   SUPER-MOOD   CONTENT

"I BELIEVE IN MY CAPABILITY TO CHOOSE WISELY"

Forgiveness can be a powerful tool for improving your emotional well-being and finding inner peace. By writing down your thoughts and feelings about forgiveness, you can work through the process and let go of negative emotions. While forgiveness does not necessarily mean you understand or condone the actions of others, it can help you find healing and closure. As you go through this process, be gentle with yourself and remember that healing takes time and patience.

_____

_____

_____

THINK OF A FAVORITE BOOK OR MOVIE AND DESCRIBE WHAT IT IS ABOUT AND WHAT YOU LEARNED FROM IT.

"I CAN OVERCOME ANY OBSTACLE."

COLOR THE FACE THAT BEST DESCRIBES YOUR MOOD TODAY.

I AM FEELING........................ DATE / /

HAPPY   SAD   UNAMUSED   SUPER-GOOD   CONTENT

Have you taken the time to show appreciation for those who have shared their knowledge and wisdom with you? It is important to express gratitude to those who have taught us valuable lessons.

_____

_____

_____

_____

Thinking positively will lead to better results and a better life.

"I CHOOSE TO THINK POSITIVELY TODAY. I REFUSE TO LET NEGATIVE THOUGHTS AND EMOTIONS TAKE OVER MY MIND AND DAY."

COLOR THE FACE THAT BEST DESCRIBES YOUR MOOD TODAY.

I AM FEELING.......................... DATE   /   /

HAPPY   SAD   UNAMUSED   SUPER-MOOD   CONTENT

HOW DOES BEING MINDFUL OF THE PRESENT MOMENT HELP YOU APPRECIATE THE GOOD THINGS IN LIFE?

_____

_____

_____

_____

COLOR THE FACE THAT BEST DESCRIBES YOUR MOOD TODAY.

I AM FEELING.................................. DATE ___ / ___ / ___

HAPPY   SAD   UNAMUSED   SUPER-MOOD   CONTENT

TO LISTEN TO OTHERS WITH KINDNESS AND AN OPEN MIND MEANS BEING WILLING TO CONSIDER THEIR PERSPECTIVE AND TRY TO UNDERSTAND WHERE THEY ARE COMING FROM, EVEN IF YOU DISAGREE WITH THEM.

What actions can you take to show empathy, understanding, and open-mindedness when communicating with others?

_____

_____

_____

COLOR THE FACE THAT BEST DESCRIBES YOUR MOOD TODAY.

I AM FEELING...................................... DATE   /   /

HAPPY   SAD   UNAMUSED   SUPER-MOOD   CONTENT

COMPLIMENTING A FRIEND CAN HAVE A POSITIVE IMPACT ON BOTH THE RECIPIENT AND THE PERSON GIVING THE COMPLIMENT. IT'S A SIMPLE ACT THAT CAN BRIGHTEN SOMEONE'S DAY AND IMPROVE THEIR OVERALL MOOD.

Have you had the chance to compliment a friend today? How did it make them feel?

_____

_____

_____

COLOR THE FACE THAT BEST
DESCRIBES YOUR MOOD TODAY.

I AM FEELING..................................... DATE   /   /

HAPPY   SAD   UNAMUSED   SUPER-MOOD   CONTENT

Taking the time to reflect on the positive aspects of your life, no matter how big or small can be a valuable and beneficial practice. Consider making a list of all the good things that have happened to you recently, and spend a moment thinking about your blessings. This can help you cultivate gratitude and a sense of appreciation for the good things in your life.

_____

_____

_____

_____

_____

_____

_____

COLOR THE FACE THAT BEST DESCRIBES YOUR MOOD TODAY.

I AM FEELING.............................. DATE ___ / ___ / ___

HAPPY   SAD   UNAMUSED   SUPER-MOOD   CONTENT

BREATHE

To practice deep breathing, try to be aware of your breath as often as you can throughout the day. When you focus on your breath, you bring your mind to the present moment and feel more calm and aware. When you inhale, imagine you are smelling a beautiful flower, and when you exhale, imagine you are blowing out the candles on a birthday cake. With each breath, you can release any worries or tension you might be feeling. Consistent effort leads to success.

COLOR THE FACE THAT BEST DESCRIBES YOUR MOOD TODAY.

I AM FEELING.............................. **DATE** / /

HAPPY   SAD   UNAMUSED   SUPER-MOOD   CONTENT

COLOR THE FACE THAT BEST DESCRIBES YOUR MOOD TODAY.

I AM FEELING..

HAPPY   SAD   UNAMUSED   SUPER-MOOD   CONTENT

"I am always learning."

Is there something interesting that you have learned recently that you would like to share?

What is the topic, and why do you find it fascinating?

_____

_____

_____

_____

_____

_____

_____

_____

COLOR THE FACE THAT BEST DESCRIBES YOUR MOOD TODAY.

I AM FEELING......................... DATE ___/___/___

HAPPY   SAD   UNAMUSED   SUPER-MOOD   CONTENT

WHAT ARE A FEW THINGS THAT YOU ENJOY OR APPRECIATE ABOUT YOUR SCHOOL?

"I AM GRATEFUL FOR THE ABUNDANCE OF LOVE IN MY LIFE AND KNOW I AM A VALUED AND BELOVED DAUGHTER."

COLOR THE FACE THAT BEST DESCRIBES YOUR MOOD TODAY.

I AM FEELING................................. DATE ___ / ___ / ___

HAPPY   SAD   UNAMUSED   SUPER-MOOD   CONTENT

"I Am Happy"

What kind of positive changes would you like to see in school, and how can you help make them happen?

COLOR THE FACE THAT BEST DESCRIBES YOUR MOOD TODAY.

I AM FEELING.................... DATE   /   /

HAPPY   SAD   UNAMUSED   SUPER-MOOD   CONTENT

IMAGINE YOURSELF TRAVELING TO ANY COUNTRY IN THE WORLD. WHICH ONE WOULD YOU CHOOSE, AND WHAT DRAWS YOU TO IT?

_____

_____

_____

_____

_____

_____

_____

_____

_____

COLOR THE FACE THAT BEST DESCRIBES YOUR MOOD TODAY.

I AM FEELING........................... DATE ___/___/___

HAPPY   SAD   UNAMUSED   SUPER-NOOD   CONTENT

WRITE ABOUT ANY THOUGHTS, IDEAS, OR FEELINGS YOU WANT TO EXPRESS OR SHARE.

_____

_____

_____

_____

COLOR THE FACE THAT BEST DESCRIBES YOUR MOOD TODAY.

I AM FEELING.........................   DATE   /   /

HAPPY   SAD   UNAMUSED   SUPER-MOOD   CONTENT

Fill the jar with Gratitude.

Write down one word that represents something you are thankful for on a small envelope in the jar. This way, you are creating a jar filled with words that represent your gratitude and appreciation for the things in your life. As you add more words to the envelopes, the jar becomes a visual representation of all the things you are thankful for. This can be a fun and uplifting activity that helps you focus on the positive aspects of your life and cultivate gratefulness.

COLOR THE FACE THAT BEST DESCRIBES YOUR MOOD TODAY.

I AM FEELING.. DATE ___ / ___ / ___

HAPPY   SAD   UNAMUSED   SUPER-MOOD   CONTENT

WHAT ENCOURAGES YOU TO GIVE IT YOUR ALL?

_____

_____

_____

COLOR THE FACE THAT BEST
DESCRIBES YOUR MOOD TODAY.

I AM FEELING.......................... **DATE** ___ / ___ / ___

HAPPY   SAD   UNAMUSED   SUPER-GOOD   CONTENT

THINK ABOUT A MISTAKE THAT YOU ARE GRATEFUL FOR HAVING MADE AND EXPLAIN WHAT YOU LEARNED FROM THE EXPERIENCE.

COLOR THE FACE THAT BEST DESCRIBES YOUR MOOD TODAY.

I AM FEELING.. DATE   /   /

HAPPY   SAD   UNAMUSED   SUPER-MOOD   CONTENT

COLOR THE FACE THAT BEST
DESCRIBES YOUR MOOD TODAY.

I AM FEELING.................................... DATE   /   /

😊 HAPPY   ☹️ SAD   😐 UNAMUSED   😄 SUPER-MOOD   😉 CONTENT

Think about a family member
who brings joy to your life.
What are their specific actions
or qualities that make you
happy?

What's something you've always wanted to change in your life, and what impact do you think it would have on your overall happiness?

_____

_____

_____

"MY FAILURES ARE OPPORTUNITIES FOR GROWTH AND LEARNING."

COLOR THE FACE THAT BEST DESCRIBES YOUR MOOD TODAY.

I AM FEELING........................... DATE   /   /

HAPPY   SAD   UNAMUSED   SUPER-MOOD   CONTENT

What are some ways that you can reward yourself for your hard work and accomplishments?

☐ _____

☐ _____

☐ _____

"THERE IS NO TIME LIKE THE PRESENT!"

COLOR THE FACE THAT BEST DESCRIBES YOUR MOOD TODAY.

I AM FEELING.......................... DATE ___ / ___ / ___

HAPPY   SAD   UNAMUSED   SUPER-GOOD   CONTENT

How are you feeling today? Can you think of events or thoughts that have made you feel a certain way? Is there a particular reason why these things have affected you?

_____

_____

_____

_____

"I trust in my own strength and capability to succeed in anything I put my effort towards. I embrace challenges with a positive attitude and know they will help me grow. I appreciate and acknowledge my own personal strength and accomplishments."

COLOR THE FACE THAT BEST DESCRIBES YOUR MOOD TODAY.

I AM FEELING.......................... DATE   /   /

HAPPY   SAD   UNAMUSED   SUPER-GOOD   CONTENT

COLOR THE FACE THAT BEST DESCRIBES YOUR MOOD TODAY.

I AM FEELING.. DATE   /   /   _____

HAPPY   SAD   UNAMUSED   SUPER-MOOD   CONTENT

BY PAYING ATTENTION TO A FEW KEY AREAS IN YOUR DAILY LIFE, YOU CAN TAKE STEPS TO IMPROVE YOUR OVERALL WELL-BEING. HERE ARE A FEW THINGS TO CONSIDER:

- Pay attention to your thoughts and feelings, and take a few minutes to relax and de-stress when you're feeling overwhelmed.
- Get enough sleep each night and make an effort to eat healthy foods. These habits will help you feel more energized and focused.
- Take some time each day to do something you enjoy, whether it's reading, spending time with loved ones, or engaging in a hobby. This will help reduce stress and boost your happiness.

_____

_____

_____

_____

COLOR THE FACE THAT BEST DESCRIBES YOUR MOOD TODAY.

I AM FEELING.................................... DATE   /   /

HAPPY   SAD   UNAMUSED   SUPER-MOOD   CONTENT

IS THERE ANYTHING THAT HAS BEEN TOUGH FOR YOU TO DEAL WITH LATELY? HOW HAVE YOU TRIED TO HANDLE IT? HAVE YOU TALKED TO ANYONE ABOUT IT?

"I AM IN CONTROL OF MY HAPPINESS. I DECIDE HOW I WANT TO FEEL AND WHAT ACTIONS I NEED TO TAKE IN ORDER TO MAINTAIN A POSITIVE OUTLOOK AND IMPROVE MY MOOD. HAPPINESS IS A CHOICE THAT I MAKE EVERY DAY."

LOVE

WHAT MAKES YOU FEEL HAPPY AND FULFILLED IN LIFE?

_____

_____

_____

_____

_____

_____

WHAT ARE SOME THINGS YOU BELIEVE ARE IMPORTANT TO ACHIEVE IN YOUR LIFE, AND HOW DO THEY RELATE TO YOUR PERSONAL VALUES?

_____

_____

_____

_____

_____

COLOR THE FACE THAT BEST DESCRIBES YOUR MOOD TODAY.

I AM FEELING........................... DATE   /   /

HAPPY   SAD   UNAMUSED   SUPER-MOOD   CONTENT

CAN YOU THINK OF THREE THINGS THAT CONTRIBUTED TO A POSITIVE OR ENJOYABLE EXPERIENCE TODAY?

_____

_____

_____

_____

"I AM FORTUNATE TO HAVE PEOPLE IN MY LIFE WHO CONSISTENTLY SHOW ME LOVE AND RESPECT EVERY DAY."

COLOR THE FACE THAT BEST DESCRIBES YOUR MOOD TODAY.

I AM FEELING............................ DATE ___/___/___

HAPPY   SAD   UNAMUSED   SUPER-MOOD   CONTENT

I CAN'T WAIT TO...

- [ ]
- [ ]
- [ ]
- [ ]
- [ ]
- [ ]

"I BELIEVE IN MYSELF AND MY ABILITIES TO ACHIEVE MY GOALS."

COLOR THE FACE THAT BEST DESCRIBES YOUR MOOD TODAY.

I AM FEELING.............................. DATE ___ / ___ / ___

HAPPY   SAD   UNAMUSED   SUPER-GOOD   CONTENT

"LIFE IS A DANCE. MINDFULNESS IS WITNESSING THAT DANCE."
~ AMIT RAY

WHAT IS SOMETHING THAT SCARES YOU, AND HOW CAN YOU WORK TOWARDS FACING AND OVERCOMING THAT FEAR?

COLOR THE FACE THAT BEST DESCRIBES YOUR MOOD TODAY.

I AM FEELING................................. DATE ___ / ___ / ___

HAPPY   SAD   UNAMUSED   SUPER-NOOU   CONTENT

It's completely normal not to have all the answers. No one can be expected to know everything, and that's okay. The important thing is to have the desire to learn and grow. As long as you're actively working towards personal development, you're on the right path.

WHEN I GROW UP, I WANT TO...

_____
_____
_____
_____

"I AM DEEPLY COMMITTED TO MY GOALS AND DREAMS AND WILL DO WHATEVER IT TAKES TO ACHIEVE THEM. I AM DRIVEN BY PASSION AND REFUSE TO GIVE UP OR GIVE IN, EVEN WHEN FACED WITH CHALLENGES. I THINK THAT ANYTHING WORTH DOING TAKES HARD WORK AND PERSISTENCE, AND I'M READY TO PUT IN THE EFFORT I NEED TO SUCCEED. MY PASSION AND RESILIENCE WILL GUIDE ME TOWARDS REALIZING MY ASPIRATIONS."

YOU ARE *amazing*

COLOR THE FACE THAT BEST DESCRIBES YOUR MOOD TODAY.

I AM FEELING................................... DATE / /

HAPPY   SAD   UNAMUSED   SUPER-MOOD   CONTENT

As you reach the end of this book, take some time to reflect on all that you have learned and discovered about yourself and others.

Remember that it's okay not to have all the answers and that personal growth is a continuous process.

Be patient with yourself and others, and always strive to learn and grow.

Trust that you are on the right path and that every new experience, good or bad, is an opportunity for growth and self-discovery.

Keep an open heart and an open mind, and remember that the journey is just as important as the destination.

Made in United States
Orlando, FL
11 October 2024

52555067R00070